Contents

Functions of the United States Patent and Trademark Office...1
What Are Patents, Trademarks, Servicemarks, and Copyrights?..1
What Is a Patent?..1
    What Is a Copyright?..2
Patent Laws..2
What Can Be Patented..2
Novelty And Non-Obviousness, Conditions For Obtaining A Patent 3
The United States Patent And Trademark Office 3
General Information and Correspondence 5
Public Search Facility and Patent and Trademark Depository Libraries 6
Provisional Application for Patent...8
Independent Inventor Resources 8
Who May Apply For A Patent 8
Application For Patent 9
    Non-Provisional Application for a Patent...9
    Provisional Application for a Patent 10
    Publication of Patent Applications...11
File Your Application Electronicly Using EFS-Web 11
Oath or Declaration, Signature 12
Filing, Search, and Examination Fees..13
Specification (Description and Claims) 13
Drawing..15
    Standards for Drawings..15
    Models, Exhibits, And Specimens 20
Examination of Applications and Proceedings in the 20
United States Patent and Trademark Office..20
    Restrictions 21
    Office Action 21
    Applicant's Reply 21
    Final Rejection 21
    Amendments to Application 22
Appeal to the Board of Patent Appeals and Interferences and to the Courts.....................................23
Allowance and Issue of Patent..24
Patent Term Extension and Adjustment 24

Nature of Patent and Patent Rights 25
Maintenance Fees 25
Correction of Patents 26
Assignments and Licenses 26
Recording of Assignments 26
Joint Ownership 27
Infringement of Patents 27
Patent Marking and Patent Pending 27
Design Patents 28
Plant Patents 28
Treaties and Foreign Patents 29
Foreign Applicants for U.S. Patents 30

General Information Concerning Patents

Functions of the United States Patent and Trademark Office

The United States Patent and Trademark Office (USPTO or Office) is an agency of the U.S. Department of Commerce. The role of the USPTO is to grant patents for the protection of inventions and to register trademarks. It serves the interest of inventors and businesses with respect to their inventions and corporate products, and service identifications. It also advises and assists the President of the United States, the Secretary of Commerce, the bureaus and offices of the Department of Commerce and other agencies of the government in matters involving all domestic and global aspects of "intellectual property." Through the preservation, classification, and dissemination of patent information, the Office promotes the industrial and technological progress of the nation and strengthens the economy.

In discharging its patent related duties, the USPTO examines applications and grants patents on inventions when applicants are entitled to them; it publishes and disseminates patent information, records assignments of patents, maintains search files of U.S. and foreign patents, and maintains a search room for public use in examining issued patents and records. The Office supplies copies of patents and official records to the public. It provides training to practitioners as to requirements of the patent statutes and regulations, and it publishes the Manual of Patent Examining Procedure to elucidate these. Similar functions are performed relating to trademarks. By protecting intellectual endeavors and encouraging technological progress, the USPTO seeks to preserve the United States' technological edge, which is key to our current and future competitiveness. The USPTO also disseminates patent and trademark information that promotes an understanding of intellectual property protection and facilitates the development and sharing of new technologies worldwide.

What Are Patents, Trademarks, Servicemarks, and Copyrights?

Some people confuse patents, copyrights, and trademarks. Although there may be some similarities among these kinds of intellectual property protection, they are different and serve different purposes.

What Is a Patent?

A patent for an invention is the grant of a property right to the inventor, issued by the United States Patent and Trademark Office. Generally, the term of a new patent is 20 years from the date on which the application for the patent was filed in the United States or, in special cases, from the date an earlier related application was filed, subject to the payment of maintenance fees. U.S. patent grants are effective only within the United States, U.S. territories, and U.S. possessions. Under certain circumstances, patent term extensions or adjustments may be available.

The right conferred by the patent grant is, in the language of the statute and of the grant itself, "the right to exclude others from making, using, offering for sale, or selling" the invention in the United States or "importing" the invention into the United States. What is granted is not the right to make, use, offer for sale, sell or import, but the right to exclude others from making, using, offering for sale, selling or importing the invention. Once a patent is issued, the patentee must enforce the patent without aid of the USPTO.

There are three types of patents:

1) **Utility patents** may be granted to anyone who invents or discovers any new and useful process, machine, article of manufacture, or composition of matter, or any new and useful improvement thereof;

2) **Design patents** may be granted to anyone who invents a new, original, and ornamental design for an article of manufacture; and

3) **Plant patents** may be granted to anyone who invents or discovers and asexually reproduces any distinct and new variety of plant.

What Is a Trademark or Servicemark?

A trademark is a word, name, symbol, or device that is used in trade with goods to indicate the source of the goods and to distinguish them from the goods of others. A servicemark is the same as a trademark except that it identifies and distinguishes the source of a service rather than a product. The terms "trademark" and "mark" are commonly used to refer to both trademarks and servicemarks.

Trademark rights may be used to prevent others from using a confusingly similar mark, but not to prevent others from making the same goods or from selling the same goods or services under a clearly different mark. Trademarks which are used in interstate or foreign commerce may be registered with the USPTO. The registration procedure for trademarks and general information concerning trademarks is described on a separate page entitled "Basic Facts about Trademarks" (*http://www.uspto.gov/web/offices/tac/doc/basic/*).

What Is a Copyright?

Copyright is a form of protection provided to the authors of "original works of authorship" including literary, dramatic, musical, artistic, and certain other intellectual works, both published and unpublished. The 1976 Copyright Act generally gives the owner of copyright the exclusive right to reproduce the copyrighted work, to prepare derivative works, to distribute copies or phonorecords of the copyrighted work, to perform the copyrighted work publicly, or to display the copyrighted work publicly.

The copyright protects the form of expression rather than the subject matter of the writing. For example, a description of a machine could be copyrighted, but this would only prevent others from copying the description; it would not prevent others from writing a description of their own or from making and using the machine. Copyrights are registered by the *Copyright Office of the Library of Congress*.

Patent Laws

The Constitution of the United States gives Congress the power to enact laws relating to patents, in Article I, section 8, which reads "Congress shall have power . . . to promote the progress of science and useful arts, by securing for limited times to authors and inventors the exclusive right to their respective writings and discoveries." Under this power Congress has from time to time enacted various laws relating to patents. The first patent law was enacted in 1790. The patent laws underwent a general revision which was enacted July 19, 1952, and which came into effect January 1, 1953. It is codified in Title 35, United States Code. Additionally, on November 29, 1999, Congress enacted the American Inventors Protection Act of 1999 (AIPA), which further revised the patent laws. See Public Law 106-113, 113 Stat. 1501 (1999).

The patent law specifies the subject matter for which a patent may be obtained and the conditions for patentability. The law establishes the United States Patent and Trademark Office to administer the law relating to the granting of patents and contains various other provisions relating to patents.

What Can Be Patented

The patent law specifies the general field of subject matter that can be patented and the conditions under which a patent may be obtained.

In the language of the statute, any person who "invents or discovers any new and useful process, machine, manufacture, or composition of matter, or any new and useful improvement thereof, may obtain a patent," subject to the conditions and requirements of the law. The word "process" is defined by law as a process, act or method, and primarily includes industrial or technical processes. The term "machine" used in the statute needs no explanation. The term "manufacture" refers to articles that are made, and includes all manufactured articles. The term "composition of matter" relates to chemical compositions and may include mixtures of ingredients as well as new chemical compounds. These classes of subject matter taken together include practically everything that is made by man and the processes for making the products.

The Atomic Energy Act of 1954 excludes the patenting of inventions useful solely in the utilization of special nuclear material or atomic energy in an atomic weapon. See 42 U.S.C. 2181(a).

The patent law specifies that the subject matter must be "useful." The term "useful" in this connection refers to the condition that the subject matter has a useful purpose and also includes operativeness, that is, a machine which will not operate to perform the intended purpose would not be called useful, and therefore would not be granted a patent.

Interpretations of the statute by the courts have defined the limits of the field of subject matter that can be patented, thus it has been held that the laws of nature, physical phenomena, and abstract ideas are not patentable subject matter.

A patent cannot be obtained upon a mere idea or suggestion. The patent is granted upon the new machine, manufacture, etc., as has been said, and not upon the idea or suggestion of the new machine. A complete description of the actual machine or other subject matter for which a patent is sought is required.

Novelty And Non-Obviousness, Conditions For Obtaining A Patent

In order for an invention to be patentable it must be new as defined in the patent law, which provides that an invention cannot be patented if: "(a) the invention was known or used by others in this country, or patented or described in a printed publication in this or a foreign country, before the invention thereof by the applicant for patent," or "(b) the invention was patented or described in a printed publication in this or a foreign country or in public use or on sale in this country more than one year prior to the application for patent in the United States . . ."

If the invention has been described in a printed publication anywhere in the world, or if it was known or used by others in this country before the date that the applicant made his/her invention, a patent cannot be obtained. If the invention has been described in a printed publication anywhere, or has been in public use or on sale in this country more than one year before the date on which an application for patent is filed in this country, a patent cannot be obtained. In this connection it is immaterial when the invention was made, or whether the printed publication or public use was by the inventor himself/herself or by someone else. If the inventor describes the invention in a printed publication or uses the invention publicly, or places it on sale, he/she must apply for a patent before one year has gone by, otherwise any right to a patent will be lost. The inventor must file on the date of public use or disclosure, however, in order to preserve patent rights in many foreign countries.

Even if the subject matter sought to be patented is not exactly shown by the prior art, and involves one or more differences over the most nearly similar thing already known, a patent may still be refused if the differences would be obvious. The subject matter sought to be patented must be sufficiently different from what has been used or described before that it may be said to be nonobvious to a person having ordinary skill in the area of technology related to the invention. For example, the substitution of one color for another, or changes in size, are ordinarily not patentable.

The United States Patent And Trademark Office

Congress established the United States Patent and Trademark Office (USPTO or Office) to issue patents on behalf of the government. The Patent Office as a distinct bureau dates from the year 1802 when a separate official in the Department of State who became known as "Superintendent of Patents" was placed in charge of patents. The revision of the patent laws enacted in 1836 reorganized the Patent Office and designated the official in charge as Commissioner of Patents. The Patent Office remained in the

Department of State until 1849 when it was transferred to the Department of Interior. In 1925 it was transferred to the Department of Commerce where it is today. The name of the Patent Office was changed to the Patent and Trademark Office in 1975 and changed to the United States Patent and Trademark Office in 2000.

The USPTO administers the patent laws as they relate to the granting of patents for inventions, and performs other duties relating to patents. Applications for patents are examined to determine if the applicants are entitled to patents under the law and patents are granted when applicants are so entitled. The USPTO publishes issued patents and most patent applications 18 months from the earliest effective application filing date, and makes various other publications concerning patents. The USPTO also records assignments of patents, maintains a search room for the use of the public to examine issued patents and records, and supplies copies of records and other papers, and the like. Similar functions are performed with respect to the registration of trademarks. The USPTO has no jurisdiction over questions of infringement and the enforcement of patents.

The head of the Office is the Under Secretary of Commerce for Intellectual Property and Director of the United States Patent and Trademark Office (Director). The Director's staff includes the Deputy Under Secretary of Commerce and Deputy Director of the USPTO, the Commissioner for Patents, the Commissioner for Trademarks, and other officials. As head of the Office, the Director superintends or performs all duties respecting the granting and issuing of patents and the registration of trademarks; exercises general supervision over the entire work of the USPTO; prescribes the rules, subject to the approval of the Secretary of Commerce, for the conduct of proceedings in the USPTO, and for recognition of attorneys and agents; decides various questions brought before the Office by petition as prescribed by the rules; and performs other duties necessary and required for the administration of the United States Patent and Trademark Office.

The work of examining applications for patents is divided among a number of examining technology centers (TC), each TC having jurisdiction over certain assigned fields of technology. Each TC is headed by group directors and staffed by examiners and support staff. The examiners review applications for patents and determine whether patents can be granted. An appeal can be taken to the Board of Patent Appeals and Interferences from their decisions refusing to grant a patent, and a review by the Director of the USPTO may be had on other matters by petition. The examiners also identify applications that claim the same invention and may initiate proceedings, known as interferences, to determine who was the first inventor.

In addition to the examining TCs, other offices perform various services, such as receiving and distributing mail, receiving new applications, handling sales of printed copies of patents, making copies of records, inspecting drawings, and recording assignments.

At present, the USPTO has over 6,500 employees, of whom about half are examiners and others with technical and legal training. Patent applications are received at the rate of over 450,000 per year.

In fiscal year 2011, about 93% of all patent applications received were filed electronically using the USPTO's electronic filing system called EFS-Web. It is anticipated that in fiscal year 2012, significantly more than 93% of all applications will be filed via EFS-Web. The reason for the expected increase in EFS-Web filings is that effective November 15, 2011, any regular nonprovisional utility application filed by mail or hand-delivery will require payment of an additional $400 fee called the "non-electronic filing fee", which is reduced by 50% (to $200) for applicants that qualify for small entity status under 37 CFR 1.27(a). This fee is required by Section 10(h) of the Leahy-Smith America Invents Act, Public Law 112-29 (Sept. 16, 2011; 125 Stat. 284). **The only way to avoid having to pay the additional $400 non-electronic filing fee is to file the regular nonprovisional utility patent application via EFS-Web.** Design, plant, and provisional applications are not subject to the additional non-electronic filing fee and may continue to be filed by mail or hand-delivery without additional charge. See the information available at http://www.uspto.gov/patents/process/file/efs/index.jsp. **Any questions regarding filing applications via EFS-Web should be directed to the Electronic Business Center at 866-217-9197.**

General Information and Correspondence

All business with the United States Patent and Trademark Office (USPTO or Office) should be transacted in writing. **Regular nonprovisional utility applications must be filed via EFS-Web in order to avoid the additional $400 non-electronic filing fee.** Other patent correspondence, including design, plant, and provisional application filings, as well as correspondence filed in a nonprovisional application after the application filing date (known as **"follow-on" correspondence**), can still be filed by mail or hand-delivery without incurring the $400 non-electronic filing fee. Such other correspondence relating to patent matters should be addressed to "**COMMISSIONER FOR PATENTS, P.O. Box 1450; Alexandria, VA 22313-1450**" when sent by mail via the United States Postal Service. If a mail stop is appropriate, the mail stop should also be used. Mail addressed to different mail stops should be mailed separately to ensure proper routing. For example, after final correspondence should be mailed to "Mail Stop AF; Commissioner for Patents; P.O. Box 1450; Alexandria, VA 22313-1450," and assignments should be mailed to "Mail Stop Assignment Recordation Services, Director of the U.S. Patent and Trademark Office; P.O. Box 1450; Alexandria, VA 22313-1450." Correspondents should be sure to include their full return addresses, including zip codes. The principal location of the USPTO is 600 Dulany Street, Alexandria, Virginia. The personal presence of applicants at the USPTO is unnecessary.

You do not have to be a Registered eFiler to file a patent application via EFS-Web. However, unless you are a Registered eFiler, you must not attempt to file follow-on correspondence via EFS-Web, because **Unregistered eFilers are not permitted to file follow-on correspondence via EFS-Web.** Follow-on correspondence filed by anyone other than an EFS-Web Registered eFiler must be sent by mail or hand-delivered to the address specified in the paragraph above.

Applicants and attorneys are required to conduct their business with decorum and courtesy. Papers presented in violation of this requirement will be returned.

Separate letters (but not necessarily in separate envelopes) should be written for each distinct subject of inquiry, such as assignments, payments, orders for printed copies of patents, orders for copies of records, and requests for other services. None of these inquiries should be included with letters responding to Office actions in applications.

When a letter concerns a patent application, the correspondent must include the application number (consisting of the series code and the serial number, e.g., 12/123,456) or the serial number and filing date assigned to that application by the Office, or the international application number of the international application number of the international application. When a letter concerns a patent (other than for purposes of payment of a maintenance fee), it should include the name of the patentee, the title of the invention, the patent number, and the date of issue.

An order for a copy of an assignment should identify the reel and frame number where the assignment or document is recorded; otherwise, an additional charge is made for the time consumed in making the search for the assignment.

Applications for patents, which are not published or issued as patents, are not generally open to the public, and no information concerning them is released except on written authority of the applicant, his/her assignee, or his/her attorney, or when necessary to the conduct of the business of the USPTO. Patent application publications and patents and related records, including records of any decisions, the records of assignments other than those relating to assignments of unpublished patent applications, patent applications that are relied upon for priority in a patent application publication or patent, books, and other records and papers in the Office are open to the public. They may be inspected in the USPTO Search Room or copies may be ordered.

The Office cannot respond to inquiries concerning the novelty and patentability of an invention prior to the filing of an application; give advice as to possible infringement of a patent; advise of the propriety of filing an application; respond to inquiries as to whether, or to whom, any alleged invention has been patented; act as an expounder of the patent law or as counselor for individuals, except in deciding questions arising before it in regularly filed cases. Information of a general nature may be furnished either directly or by supplying or calling attention to an appropriate publication.

Public Search Facility and Patent and Trademark Depository Libraries

The Scientific and Technical Information Center of the United States Patent and Trademark Office located at 1D58 Remsen, 400 Dulany Street, Alexandria, VA, has available for public use over 120,000 volumes of scientific and technical books in various languages, about 90,000 bound volumes of periodicals devoted to science and technology, the official journals of 77 foreign patent organizations, and over 40 million foreign patents on paper, microfilm, microfiche, and CD-ROM. The Scientific and Technical Information Center is open to the public from 8:00 a.m. to 5:00 p.m., Monday through Friday except federal holidays.

The Public Search Facility located at Madison East, First Floor, 600 Dulany Street, Alexandria, VA, is where the public may search and examine U.S. patents granted since 1790 using state of the art computer workstations. A complete patent backfile in numeric sequence is available on microfilm or in optical disc format. Official Gazettes, Annual Indexes (of Inventors), the Manual of Classification and its subject matter index, and other search aids are available in various formats. Patent assignment records of transactions affecting the ownership of patents, microfilmed deeds, and indexes are also available.

The Public Search Facility is open from 8 a.m. to 8 p.m. Monday through Friday except on federal holidays.

Many inventors attempt to make their own search of the prior patents and publications before applying for a patent. This may be done in the Public Search Facility of the USPTO, and in libraries, located throughout the United States, which have been designated as Patent and Trademark Depository Libraries (PTDLs). An inventor may make a preliminary search through the U.S. patents and publications to discover if the particular invention or one similar to it has been shown in the prior patent. An inventor may also employ patent attorneys or agents to perform the preliminary search. This search may not be as complete as that made by the USPTO during the examination of an application, but only serves, as its name indicates, a preliminary purpose. For this reason, the patent examiner may, and often does, reject claims in an application on the basis of prior patents or publications not found in the preliminary search.

Those who cannot come to the Public Search Facility may order from the USPTO copies of lists of original patents or of cross-referenced patents contained in the subclasses comprising the field of search, or may inspect and obtain copies of the patents at a Patent and Trademark Depository Library. The PTDLs receive current issues of U.S. patents and maintain collections of earlier issued patent and trademark information. The scope of these collections varies from library to library, ranging from patents of only recent years to all or most of the patents issued since 1790.

These patent collections are open to public use. Each of the PTDLs, in addition, offers the publications of the U.S. Patent Classification System (e.g., Manual of Classification, Index to the U.S. Patent Classification System, Classification Definitions, etc.) and other patent documents and forms, and provides technical staff assistance in their use to aid the public in gaining effective access to information contained in patents. The collections are organized in patent number sequence.

Available in all PTDLs is the Cassis CD-ROM system. With various files, it permits the effective identification of appropriate classifications to search, provides numbers of patents assigned to a classification to facilitate finding the patents in a numerical file of patents, provides the current classification(s) of all patents, permits word searching on classification titles, and on abstracts, and provides certain bibliographic information on more recently issued patents. These libraries also provide access to the USPTO web site.

Facilities for making paper copies from microfilm, the paper bound volumes or CD-ROM are generally provided for a fee.

Due to variations in the scope of patent collections among the PTDLs and in their hours of service to the public, anyone contemplating the use of the patents at a particular library is advised to contact that library, in advance, about its collection, services, and hours, so as to avert possible inconvenience. For a complete list of PTDLs, refer to the USPTO Web site at *www.uspto.gov/web/offices/ac/ido/ptdl/*.

Attorneys and Agents

The preparation of an application for patent and the conducting of the proceedings in the United States Patent and Trademark Office (USPTO or Office) to obtain the patent is an undertaking requiring the knowledge of patent law and rules and Office practice and procedures, as well as knowledge of the scientific or technical matters involved in the particular invention.

Inventors may prepare their own applications and file them in the USPTO and conduct the proceedings themselves, but unless they are familiar with these matters or study them in detail, they may get into considerable difficulty. While a patent may be obtained in many cases by persons not skilled in this work, there would be no assurance that the patent obtained would adequately protect the particular invention.

Most inventors employ the services of registered patent attorneys or patent agents. The law gives the USPTO the power to make rules and regulations governing conduct and the recognition of patent attorneys and agents to practice before the USPTO. Persons who are not recognized by the USPTO for this practice are not permitted by law to represent inventors before the USPTO. The USPTO maintains a register of attorneys and agents. To be admitted to this register, a person must comply with the regulations prescribed by the Office, which require a showing that the person is of good moral character and of good repute and that he/she has the legal, and scientific and technical qualifications necessary to render applicants for patents a valuable service. Certain of these qualifications must be demonstrated by the passing of an examination. Those admitted to the examination must have a college degree in engineering or physical science or the equivalent of such a degree.

The USPTO registers both attorneys at law and persons who are not attorneys at law. The former persons are now referred to as "patent attorneys" and the latter persons are referred to as "patent agents." Both patent attorneys and patent agents are permitted to prepare an application for a patent and conduct the prosecution in the USPTO. Patent agents, however, cannot conduct patent litigation in the courts or perform various services which the local jurisdiction considers as practicing law. For example, a patent agent could not draw up a contract relating to a patent, such as an assignment or a license, if the state in which he/she resides considers drafting contracts as practicing law.

Some individuals and organizations that are not registered advertise their services in the fields of patent searching and invention marketing and development. Such individuals and organizations cannot represent inventors before the USPTO. They are not subject to USPTO discipline, but the USPTO does provide a public forum (*www.uspto.gov/web/offices/com/iip/complaints.htm*) where complaints and responses concerning invention promoters/promotion firms are published.

The USPTO cannot recommend any particular attorney or agent, or aid in the selection of an attorney or agent, as by stating, in response to inquiry that a named patent attorney, agent, or firm, is "reliable" or "capable." The USPTO maintains a directory of registered patent attorneys and agents at *http://des.uspto.gov/OEDCI*.

The telephone directories of most large cities have, in the classified section, a heading for patent attorneys under which those in that area are listed. Many large cities have associations of patent attorneys.

In employing a patent attorney or agent, the inventor executes a power of attorney which is filed in the USPTO and made of record in the application file. When a registered attorney or agent has been appointed, the Office does not communicate with the inventor directly but conducts the correspondence with the attorney or agent since he/she is acting for the inventor thereafter although the inventor is free to contact the USPTO concerning the status of his/her application. The inventor may remove the attorney or agent by revoking the power of attorney.

The USPTO has the power to disbar, or suspend from practicing before it, persons guilty of gross misconduct, etc., but this can only be done after a full hearing with the presentation of clear and convincing evidence concerning the misconduct. The USPTO will receive and, in appropriate cases, act upon complaints against attorneys and agents. The fees charged to inventors by patent attorneys and agents for their professional services are not subject to regulation by the USPTO. Definite evidence of overcharging may afford basis for USPTO action, but the Office rarely intervenes in disputes concerning fees.

Provisional Application for Patent

Inventors also have the option of filing a Provisional Application for Patent. Provisional applications are described in more detail below. To receive more information on provisional applications, please visit the USPTO Web site or request a print brochure by calling 800-786-9199 or 571-272-1000.

Independent Inventor Resources

A section of the USPTO's Web site (*http://www.uspto.gov/inventors/index.jsp*) is devoted to independent inventors (site is entitled "Inventors Resources") and offers a broad range of material covering most aspects of the patent and trademark process. The Web site also endeavors to educate independent inventors about fraudulent invention development and marketing firms and the scams that may affect these inventors and offers tips and warning signs on avoiding these scams. The site also publishes complaints against these firms and any
responses received from them. The site further provides links to other USPTO sites, as well as links to other federal agencies.

Mail for the Inventor's Assistance Program, including complaints about Invention Promoters should be addressed to:

Mail Stop 24
Director of the U.S. Patent and Trademark Office
P.O. Box 1450
Alexandria, VA 22313-1450
E-mail: *independentinventor@uspto.gov*

The Inventors Assistance Center (IAC) provides the primary point of contact to the independent inventor community and the general public for general information about filing a disclosure document, a provisional patent application, or a regular, non-provisional patent application.

For additional information on the patent process, telephone the Inventors Assistance Center at:

Telephone 1-800-PTO-9199
TTY: 571-272-9950
USPTO's home page is *http://www.uspto.gov*.

Who May Apply For A Patent

According to the law, only the inventor may apply for a patent, with certain exceptions. If a person who is not the inventor should apply for a patent, the patent, if it were obtained, would be invalid. The person applying in such a case who falsely states that he/she is the inventor would also be subject to criminal penalties. If the inventor is dead, the application may be made by legal representatives, that is, the administrator or executor of the estate. If the inventor is insane, the application for patent may be made by a legal representative (e.g., guardian). If an inventor refuses to apply for a patent or cannot be found, a joint inventor or, if there is no joint inventor available, a person having a proprietary interest in the invention may apply on behalf of the non-signing inventor.

If two or more persons make an invention jointly, they apply for a patent as joint inventors. A person who makes only a financial contribution is not a joint inventor and cannot be joined in the application as an inventor. It is possible to correct an innocent mistake in erroneously omitting an inventor or in erroneously naming a person as an inventor.

Officers and employees of the United States Patent and Trademark Office are prohibited by law from applying for a patent or acquiring, directly or indirectly, except by inheritance or bequest, any patent or any right or interest in any patent.

Application For Patent

Non-Provisional Application for a Patent

A nonprovisional application for a patent is made to the Director of the United States Patent and Trademark Office and includes:

(1) A written document which comprises a specification (description and claims);

(2) Drawings (when necessary);

(3) An oath or declaration; and

(4) Filing, search, and examination fees. Applicant must determine that small entity status is appropriate before making an assertion of entitlement to small entity status and paying a small entity fee. Fees change each October. The fee schedule is posted on the USPTO Web site. Note that by filing electronically via EFS-Web, the filing fee for an applicant qualifying for small entity status is reduced by 50%. That's a savings of almost $100 compared to the filing fee for a small entity applicant who files his or her application in paper.

Effective November 15, 2011, any regular nonprovisional utility application filed by mail or hand-delivery will require payment of an additional $400 fee called the "non-electronic filing fee", which is reduced by 50% (to $200) for applicants that qualify for small entity status under 37 CFR 1.27(a). **The only way to avoid having to pay the additional $400 non-electronic filing fee is by filing the regular nonprovisional utility application via EFS-Web.** A small entity applicant who files electronically not only avoids the additional non-electronic filing fee ($200 for small entity applicants), the small entity applicant who files electronically also receives a 50% discount on the regular filing fee as discussed in the paragraph above. **Effective November 15, 2011, the total savings to the small entity applicant who files electronically is almost $300!**

Other patent correspondence, including design, plant, and provisional application filings, as well as correspondence filed in a nonprovisional application after the application filing date (known as **"follow-on" correspondence**), can still be filed by mail or hand-delivery without incurring the $400 non-electronic filing fee. You do not have to be a Registered eFiler to file a patent application via EFS-Web. However, unless you are a Registered eFiler, you must not attempt to file follow-on correspondence via EFS-Web, because **Unregistered eFilers are not permitted to file follow-on correspondence via EFS-Web**. Follow-on correspondence filed by anyone other than an EFS-Web Registered eFiler must be sent by mail or be hand-delivered. (See the "General Information and Correspondence" section of this brochure.) In the event you receive from the USPTO a "Notice of Incomplete Application" in response to your EFS-Web filing stating that an application number has been assigned but no filing date has been granted, you must become a Registered eFiler and file your reply to the "Notice of Incomplete Application" via EFS-Web in order to avoid the $400 non-electronic filing fee. To become a Registered eFiler and have the ability to file follow-on correspondence, please consult the information at http://www.uspto.gov/patents/process/file/efs/guidance/register.jsp, or call the Electronic Business Center at 866-217-9197.

The specification (description and claims) can be created using a word processing program such as Microsoft® Word or Corel® WordPerfect. The document containing the specification can normally be converted into PDF format by the word processing program itself so that it can be included as an attachment when filing the application via EFS-Web. Other application documents, such as drawings and a hand-signed declaration, may have to be scanned as a PDF file for filing via EFS-Web. See the information available at http://www.uspto.gov/patents/process/file/efs/index.jsp. **Any questions**

regarding filing applications via EFS-Web should be directed to the Electronic Business Center at 866-217-9197.

All application documents must be in the English language or a translation into the English language will be required along with the required fee set forth in 37 CFR 1.17(i).

Each document (which should be filed via EFS-Web in PDF format) must have a top margin of at least 2.0 cm (3/4 inch), a left side margin of at least 2.5 cm (1 inch), a right side margin of at least 2.0 cm (3/4 inch) and a bottom margin of at least 2.0 cm (3/4 inch) with no holes made in the submitted papers. It is also required that the spacing on all papers be 1 1/2 or double-spaced and the application papers must be numbered consecutively (centrally located above or below the text) starting with page one.

The specification must have text written in a nonscript font (e.g., Arial, Times Roman, or Courier, preferably a font size of 12) lettering style having capital letters which should be at least 0.3175 cm (0.125 inch) high, but may be no smaller than 0.21 cm (0.08 inch) high (e.g., a font size of 6). The specification must have only a single column of text.

The specification must conclude with a claim or claims particularly pointing out and distinctly claiming the subject matter which the applicant regards as the invention. The portion of the application in which the applicant sets forth the claim or claims is an important part of the application, as it is the claims that define the scope of the protection afforded by the patent. The claims must commence on a separate sheet.

More than one claim may be presented provided they differ from each other. Claims may be presented in independent form (e.g. the claim stands by itself) or in dependent form, referring back to and further limiting another claim or claims in the same application. Any dependent claim which refers back to more than one other claim is considered a "multiple dependent claim."

The application for patent is not forwarded for examination until all required parts, complying with the rules related thereto, are received. If any application is filed without all the required parts for obtaining a filing date (incomplete or defective), the applicant will be notified of the deficiencies and given a time period to complete the application filing (a surcharge may be required)—at which time a filing date as of the date of such a completed submission will be obtained by the applicant. If the omission is not corrected within a specified time period, the application will be returned or otherwise disposed of; the filing fee if submitted will be refunded less a handling fee as set forth in the fee schedule.

The filing fee and declaration or oath need not be submitted with the parts requiring a filing date. It is, however, desirable that all parts of the complete application be deposited in the Office together; otherwise each part must be signed and a letter must accompany each part, accurately and clearly connecting it with the other parts of the application. If an application which has been accorded a filing date does not include the filing fee or the oath/declaration, applicant will be notified and given a time period to pay the filing fee, file an oath/declaration and pay a surcharge.

All applications received in the USPTO are numbered in sequential order and the applicant will be informed of the application number and filing date by a filing receipt.

The filing date of an application for patent is the date on which a specification (including at least one claim) and any drawings necessary to understand the subject matter sought to be patented are received in the USPTO; or the date on which the last part completing the application is received in the case of a previously incomplete or defective application.

Provisional Application for a Patent

Since June 8, 1995, the USPTO has offered inventors the option of filing a provisional application for patent which was designed to provide a lower cost first patent filing in the United States and to give U.S. applicants parity with foreign applicants. Claims and oath or declaration are NOT required for a provisional application. Provisional application provides the means to establish an early effective filing date in a patent application and permits the term "Patent Pending" to be applied in connection with the invention. Provisional applications may not be filed for design inventions.

The filing date of a provisional application is the date on which a written description of the invention, and drawings if necessary, are received in the USPTO. To be complete, a provisional application must also include the filing fee, and a cover sheet specifying that the application is a provisional application for patent. The applicant would then have up to 12 months to file a non-provisional application for patent as described above. The claimed subject matter in the later filed non-provisional application is entitled to the benefit of the filing date of the provisional application if it has support in the provisional application.

If a provisional application is not filed in English, and a non-provisional application is filed claiming benefit to the provisional application, a translation of the provisional application will be required. See title 37, Code of Federal Regulations, Section 1.78(a)(5).

Provisional applications are NOT examined on their merits. A provisional application will become abandoned by the operation of law 12 months from its filing date. The 12-month pendency for a provisional application is not counted toward the 20-year term of a patent granted on a subsequently filed non-provisional application which claims benefit of the filing date of the provisional application.

A surcharge is required for filing the basic filing fee or the cover sheet on a date later than the filing of the provisional application. Unlike nonprovisional utility applications, design, plant, and provisional applications can still be filed by mail or hand-delivery without having to pay the additional $400 **non-electronic filing fee**. Design and provisional applications can also be filed via EFS-Web. Plant applications, however, are not permitted to be filed via EFS-Web.

Publication of Patent Applications

Publication of patent applications is required by the American Inventors Protection Act of 1999 for most plant and utility patent applications filed on or after November 29, 2000. On filing of a plant or utility application on or after November 29, 2000, an applicant may request that the application not be published, but only if the invention has not been and will not be the subject of an application filed in a foreign country that requires publication 18 months after filing (or earlier claimed priority date) or under the Patent Cooperation Treaty. Publication occurs after the expiration of an 18-month period following the earliest effective filing date or priority date claimed by an application. Following publication, the application for patent is no longer held in confidence by the Office and any member of the public may request access to the entire file history of the application.

As a result of publication, an applicant may assert provisional rights. These rights provide a patentee with the opportunity to obtain a reasonable royalty from a third party that infringes a published application claim provided actual notice is given to the third party by applicant, and patent issues from the application with a substantially identical claim. Thus, damages for pre-patent grant infringement by another are now available.

File Your Application Electronically Using EFS-Web

Effective November 15, 2011, any regular nonprovisional utility application filed by mail or hand-delivery will require payment of an additional $400 fee called the "non-electronic filing fee," which is reduced by 50% (to $200) for applicants that qualify for small entity status under 37 CFR 1.27(a). **The only way to avoid having to pay the additional $400 non-electronic filing fee is by filing your nonprovisional utility application via EFS-Web.** A small entity applicant who files electronically not only avoids the additional non-electronic filing ($200 for small entity applicants), the small entity applicant who files electronically also receives a 50% discount on the regular filing fee. **For that reason, the total savings to the small entity applicant who files electronically on or after November 15, 2011 is almost $300! Any questions regarding filing applications via EFS-Web should be directed to the Electronic Business Center at 866-217-9197.**

Other patent correspondence, including design, plant, and provisional application filings, as well as correspondence filed in a nonprovisional application after the application filing date (known as **"follow-on" correspondence**), can still be filed by mail or hand-delivery without incurring the $400 non-electronic filing fee. You do not have to be a Registered eFiler to file a patent application via EFS-Web. However, unless you are a Registered eFiler, you must not attempt to file follow-on correspondence via EFS-Web, because **Unregistered eFilers are not permitted to file follow-on correspondence via EFS-Web**. Follow-on correspondence filed by anyone other than an EFS-Web Registered eFiler must be sent by mail or be hand-delivered. (See the "General Information and Correspondence" section of this brochure.) In the event you receive from the USPTO a "Notice of Incomplete Application" in response to your EFS-Web filing stating that an application number has been assigned but no filing date has been granted, you must become a Registered eFiler and file your reply to the "Notice of Incomplete Application" via EFS-Web in order to avoid the $400 non-electronic filing fee. To become a Registered eFiler and have the ability to file follow-on correspondence, please consult the information at http://www.uspto.gov/patents/process/file/efs/guidance/register.jsp, or call the Electronic Business Center at 866-217-9197.

EFS-Web allows customers to electronically file patent application documents securely via the Internet via a web page. EFS-Web is a system for submitting new applications and documents related to previously-filed patent applications. Customers prepare documents in Portable Document Format (PDF), attach the documents, validate that the PDF documents will be compatible with USPTO internal automated information systems, submit the documents, and pay fees with real-time payment processing. Some forms are available as fillable EFS-Web forms. When these fillable EFS-Web forms are used, the data entered into the forms is automatically loaded into USPTO information systems. EFS-Web can be used to submit:
(A)　New utility patent applications and fees;
(B)　New design patent applications and fees;
(C)　Provisional patent applications and fees;
(D)　Requests to enter the national stage under 35 U.S.C. 371 and fees; and
(E)　Most follow-on documents and fees for a previously filed patent application.
Further information on EFS-Web is available at ***http://www.uspto.gov/patents/process/file/efs/guidance.*** See the "Legal Framework" document on that web page for a list of correspondence that may not be filed via EFS-Web and answers to frequently asked questions.

Oath or Declaration, Signature

The oath or declaration of the applicant (inventor) is required by law for a non-provisional application. The inventor must make an oath or declaration that he/she believes himself/herself to be the original and first inventor of the subject matter of the application, and he/she must make various other statements required by law and various statements required by the USPTO rules. If an application data sheet is filed, the USPTO rules require fewer statements in the oath or declaration. See title 37, Code of Federal Regulations, Sections 1.63 and 1.76. The oath must be sworn to by the inventor before a notary public or other officer authorized to administer oaths. A declaration may be used in lieu of an oath. Oaths or declarations are required for applications involving designs, plants, and utility inventions and for reissue applications. A declaration does not need to be notarized. When filing a continuation or divisional application a copy of the oath or declaration filed in the earlier application may be used unless the continuation or divisional names an additional inventor. See 37 CFR 1.63(d).

The oath or declaration must be signed by the inventor in person, or by the person entitled by law to make application on the inventor's behalf. A full first and last name with middle initial or name, if any, and the citizenship of each inventor are required. The mailing address of each inventor and foreign priority information (if any) are also required if an application data sheet is not used.

Forms for declarations are available by calling the USPTO General Information Services at 800-786-9199 or 571-272-1000 or by accessing USPTO Web site at ***http://www.uspto.gov***, indexed under the section titled "Forms, USPTO." Most of the forms on the USPTO Website are electronically fillable and can be included in the application filed via EFS-Web without having to print the form out in order to scan it for inclusion as a PDF attachment to the application.

Filing, Search, and Examination Fees

A patent application is subject to the payment of a basic fee and additional fees that include a search fee, an examination fee, and issue fee. Consult the USPTO Web site at *http://www.uspto.gov* for the current fees. Total claims that exceed 20, and independent claims that exceed 3 are considered "excess claims" for which additional fees are due. For example, if applicant filed a total of twenty-five claims, including four independent claims, applicant would be required to pay excess claims fees for five total claims exceeding 20, and one independent claim exceeding 3. If the same applicant later filed an amendment increasing the total number of claims to twenty-nine, and the number of independent claims to six, applicant would be required to pay more excess claims fees for the four additional total claims and the two additional independent claims.

In calculating fees, a claim is singularly dependent if it incorporates by reference a single preceding claim that may be an independent or dependent claim. A multiple dependent claim or any claim depending therefrom shall be considered as separate dependent claims in accordance with the number of claims to which reference is made. In addition, if the application contains multiple dependent claims, an additional fee is required for each multiple dependent claim.

If the owner of the invention is a small entity, (an independent inventor, a small business concern or a nonprofit organization), most fees are reduced by half if small entity status is claimed. If small entity status is desired and appropriate, applicants should pay the small entity filing fee. Applicants claiming small entity status should make an investigation as to whether small entity status is appropriate before claiming such status.

Most of the fees are subject to change in October of each year.

Specification (Description and Claims)

The following order of arrangement should be observed in framing the application:
(a) Application transmittal form.

(b) Fee transmittal form.

(c) Application Data Sheet.

(d) Specification.

(e) Drawings.

(f) Executed Oath or declaration.

The specification should have the following sections, in order:

  (1) Title of the Invention.
  (2) Cross Reference to related applications (if any). (Related applications may be listed on an application data sheet, either instead of or together with being listed in the specification.)
  (3) Statement of federally sponsored research/development (if any).\
  (4) The names of the parties to a joint research agreement if the claimed invention was made as a result of activites within the scope of a joint research agreement.
  (5) Reference to a "Sequence Listing," a table, or a computer program listing appendix submitted on a compact disc and an incorporation by reference of the material on the compact disc. The total number of compact disc including duplicates and the files on each compact disc shall be specified.
  (6) Background of the Invention.

(7) Brief Summary of the Invention.

(8) Brief description of the several views of the drawing (if any).

(9) Detailed Description of the Invention.

(10) A claim or claims.

(11) Abstract of the disclosure.

(12) Sequence listing (if any).

The specification must include a written description of the invention and of the manner and process of making and using it, and is required to be in such full, clear, concise, and exact terms as to enable any person skilled in the technological area to which the invention pertains, or with which it is most nearly connected, to make and use the same.

The specification must set forth the precise invention for which a patent is solicited, in such manner as to distinguish it from other inventions and from what is old. It must describe completely a specific embodiment of the process, machine, manufacture, composition of matter, or improvement invented, and must explain the mode of operation or principle whenever applicable. The best mode contemplated by the inventor for carrying out the invention must be set forth.

In the case of an improvement, the specification must particularly point out the part or parts of the process, machine, manufacture, or composition of matter to which the improvement relates, and the description should be confined to the specific improvement and to such parts as necessarily cooperate with it or as may be necessary to a complete understanding or description of it.

The title of the invention, which should be as short and specific as possible (no more than 500 characters), should appear as a heading on the first page of the specification, if it does not otherwise appear at the beginning of the application. A brief abstract of the technical disclosure in the specification including that which is new in the art to which the invention pertains, must be set forth on a separate page preferably following the claims. The abstract should be in the form of a single paragraph of 150 words or less, under the heading "Abstract of the Disclosure."

A brief summary of the invention indicating its nature and substance, which may include a statement of the object of the invention should precede the detailed description. The summary should be commensurate with the invention as claimed and any object recited should be that of the invention as claimed.

When there are drawings, there shall be a brief description of the several views of the drawings, and the detailed description of the invention shall refer to the different views by specifying the numbers of the figures, and to the different parts by use of reference numerals.

The specification must conclude with a claim or claims particularly pointing out and distinctly claiming the subject matter that the applicant regards as the invention. The portion of the application in which the applicant sets forth the claim or claims is an important part of the application, as it is the claims that define the scope of the protection afforded by the patent and which questions of infringement are judged by the courts.

More than one claim may be presented provided they differ substantially from each other and are not unduly multiplied. One or more claims may be presented in dependent form, referring back to and further limiting another claim or claims in the same application. Any dependent claim which refers back to more than one other claim is considered a "multiple dependent claim."

Multiple dependent claims shall refer to such other claims in the alternative only. A multiple dependent claim shall not serve as a basis for any other multiple dependent claim. Claims in dependent form shall be construed to include all of the limitations of the claim incorporated by reference into the dependent claim.

A multiple dependent claim shall be construed to incorporate all the limitations of each of the particular claims in relation to which it is being considered.

The claim or claims must conform to the invention as set forth in the remainder of the specification and the terms and phrases used in the claims must find clear support or antecedent basis in the description so that the meaning of the terms in the claims may be ascertainable by reference to the description.

Drawing

The applicant for a patent will be required by law to furnish a drawing of the invention whenever the nature of the case requires a drawing to understand the invention. However, the Director may require a drawing where the nature of the subject matter admits of it; this drawing must be filed with the application. This includes practically all inventions except compositions of matter or processes, but a drawing may also be useful in the case of many processes.

The drawing must show every feature of the invention specified in the claims, and is required by the Office rules to be in a particular form. The Office specifies the size of the sheet on which the drawing is made, the type of paper, the margins, and other details relating to the making of the drawing. The reason for specifying the standards in detail is that the drawings are printed and published in a uniform style when the patent issues, and the drawings must also be such that they can be readily understood by persons using the patent descriptions.

The sheets of drawings should be numbered in consecutive Arabic numerals, starting with 1, within the sight (the usable surface). **For regular nonprovisional utility applications, these "sheets" should be contained in an electronic document in PDF format filed with the other application documents via EFS-Web.** These numbers, if present, must be placed in the middle of the top of the sheet, but not in the margin. The numbers can be placed on the right-hand side if the drawing extends too close to the middle of the top edge of the usable surface. The drawing sheet numbering must be clear and larger than the numbers used as reference characters to avoid confusion. The number of each sheet should be shown by two Arabic numerals placed on either side of an oblique line, with the first being the sheet number and the second being the total number of sheets of drawings, with no other marking.

Identifying indicia, if provided, should include the title of the invention, the inventor's name, the application number (if known), and docket number (if any). This information should be placed on the top margin of each sheet of drawings. No names or other identification will be permitted within the "sight" of the drawing. The name and telephone number of a person to call if the USPTO is unable to match the drawings to the proper application may also be provided.

Standards for Drawings

(a) **Drawings.** There are two acceptable categories for presenting drawings in utility and design patent applications:
   (1) **Black ink.** Black and white drawings are normally required. India ink, or its equivalent that secures solid black lines, must be used for drawings, or

   (2) **Color.** On rare occasions, color drawings may be necessary as the only practical medium by which to disclose the subject matter sought to be patented in a utility or design patent application or the subject matter of a statutory invention registration. The color drawings must be of sufficient quality such that all details in the drawings are reproducible in black and white in the printed patent. Color drawings are not permitted in international applications (see PCT Rule 11.13), or in an application, or copy thereof, submitted under the Office electronic filing system.

The Office will accept color drawings in utility or design patent applications and statutory invention registrations only after granting a petition filed under this paragraph explaining why the color drawings are necessary. Any such petition must include the following:

(i) The fee set forth in § 1.17(h);

(ii) Three sets of color drawings;

and

(iii) An amendment to the specification to insert (unless the specification contains or has been previously amended to contain) the following language as the first paragraph of the brief description of the drawings:

The patent or application file contains at least one drawing executed in color. Copies of this patent or patent application publication with color drawing(s) will be provided by the Office upon request and payment of the necessary fee.

(b) **Photographs.**

(1) Black and white. Photographs, including photocopies of photographs, are not ordinarily permitted in utility and design patent applications. The Office will accept photographs in utility and design patent applications, however, if photographs are the only practicable medium for illustrating the claimed invention. For example, photographs or photomicrographs of: electrophoresis gels, blots (e.g., immuno- logical, western, southern, and northern), autoradiographs, cell cultures (stained and unstained), histological tissue cross sections (stained and unstained), animals, plants, in vivo imaging, thin layer chromatography plates, crystalline structures, and, in a design patent application, ornamental effects, are acceptable. If the subject matter of the application admits of illustration by a drawing, the examiner may require a drawing in place of the photograph. The photographs must be of sufficient quality so that all details in the photographs are reproducible in the printed patent.

(2) Color photographs. Color photographs will be accepted in utility and design patent applications if the conditions for accepting color drawings and black and white photographs have been satisfied. See paragraphs (a)(2) and (b)(1) of this section.

(c) **Identification of drawings.** Identifying indicia should be provided, and if provided, should include the title of the invention, inventor's name, and application number, or docket number (if any) if an application number has not been assigned to the application. If this information is provided, it must be placed on the front of each sheet within the top margin. Each drawing sheet submitted after the filing date of an application must be identified as either "Replacement Sheet" or "New Sheet" pursuant to § 1.121(d). If a marked-up copy of any amended drawing figure including annotations indicating the changes made is filed, such marked-up copy must be clearly labeled as "Annotated Sheet" pursuant to § 1.121(d)(1).

(d) **Graphic forms in drawings.** Chemical or mathematical formulae, tables, and waveforms may be submitted as drawings and are subject to the same requirements as drawings. Each chemical or mathematical formula must be labeled as a separate figure, using brackets when necessary, to show that information is properly integrated. Each group of waveforms must be presented as a single figure, using a common vertical axis with time extending along the horizontal axis. Each individual waveform discussed in the specification must be identified with a separate letter designation adjacent to the vertical axis.

(e)   Margins. The sheets must not contain frames around the sight (i.e., the usable surface), but should have scan target points (i.e., cross-hairs) printed on two cattycorner margin corners. Each sheet must include a top margin of at least 2.5 cm. (1 inch), a left side margin of at least 2.5 cm. (1 inch), a right side margin of at least 1.5 cm. (5/8 inch), and a bottom margin of at least 1.0 cm. (3/8 inch), thereby leaving a sight no greater than 17.0 cm. by 26.2 cm. on 21.0 cm. by 29.7 cm. (DIN size A4) drawing sheets, and a sight no greater than 17.6 cm. by 24.4 cm. (6 15/16 by 9 5/8 inches) on 21.6 cm. by 27.9 cm. (8 1/2 by 11 inch) drawing sheets.

(f)   Views. The drawing must contain as many views as necessary to show the invention. The views may be plan, elevation, section, or perspective views. Detail views of portions of elements, on a larger scale if necessary, may also be used. All views of the drawing must be grouped together and arranged on the sheet(s) without wasting space, preferably in an upright position, clearly separated from one another, and must not be included in the sheets containing the specifications, claims, or abstract. Views must not be connected by projection lines and must not contain center lines. Waveforms of electrical signals may be connected by dashed lines to show the relative timing of the waveforms.

(1) Exploded views. Exploded views, with the separated parts embraced by a bracket, to show The relationship or order of assembly of various parts are permissible. When an exploded view is shown in a figure that is on the same sheet as another figure, the exploded view should be placed in brackets.

(2)   Partial views. When necessary, a view of a large machine or device in its entirety may be broken into partial views on a single sheet, or extended over several sheets if there is no loss in facility of understanding the view. Partial views drawn on separate sheets must always be capable of being linked edge to edge so that no partial view contains parts of another partial view. A smaller scale view should be included showing the whole formed by the partial views and indicating the positions of the parts shown. When a portion of a view is enlarged for magnification purposes, the view and the enlarged view must each be labeled as separate views.

(i) Where views on two or more sheets form, in effect, a single complete view, the views on the several sheets must be so arranged that the complete figure can be assembled without concealing any part of any of the views appearing on the various sheets.

(ii) A very long view may be divided into several parts placed one above the other on a single sheet. However, the relationship between the different parts must be clear and unambiguous.

(1)   (3)   Sectional views. The plane upon which a sectional view is taken should be indicated on the view from which the section is cut by a broken line. The ends of the broken line should be designated by Arabic or Roman numerals corresponding to the view number of the sectional view, and should have arrows to indicate the direction of sight. Hatching must be used to indicate section portions of an object, and must be made by regularly spaced oblique parallel lines spaced sufficiently apart to enable the lines to be distinguished without difficulty. Hatching should not impede the clear reading of the reference characters and lead lines. If it is not possible to place reference characters outside the hatched area, the hatching may be broken off wherever reference characters are inserted. Hatching must be at a substantial angle to the surrounding axes or principal lines, preferably 45°. A cross section must be set out and drawn to show all of the materials as they are shown in the view from which the cross section was taken. The parts in cross section must show proper material(s) by hatching with regularly spaced parallel oblique strokes, the space between strokes being chosen on the basis of the total area to be hatched. The various parts of a cross section of the same item should be hatched in the same manner and should accurately and graphically indicate the nature of the material(s) that is illustrated in cross section. The hatching of juxtaposed different elements must be angled in a different way. In the case of large areas, hatching may be confined to an edging drawn around the entire inside of the outline of the area to be hatched. Different types of hatching should have different conventional

meanings as regards the nature of a material seen in cross section.

(2)   (4)   Alternate position. A moved position may be shown by a broken line superimposed upon a suitable view if this can be done without crowding; otherwise, a separate view must be used for this purpose.

         (5)   Modified forms. Modified forms of construction must be shown in separate views.

(g) **Arrangement of views.** One view must not be placed upon another or within the outline of another. All views on the same sheet should stand in the same direction and, if possible, stand so that they can be read with the sheet held in an upright position. If views wider than the width of the sheet are necessary for the clearest illustration of the invention, the sheet may be turned on its side so that the top of the sheet, with the appropriate top margin to be used as the heading space, is on the right-hand side. Words must appear in a horizontal, left-to-right fashion when the page is either upright or turned so that the top becomes the right side, except for graphs utilizing standard scientific convention to denote the axis of abscissas (of X) and the axis of ordinates (of Y).

(h) **Front page view.** The drawing must contain as many views as necessary to show the invention. One of the views should be suitable for inclusion on the front page of the patent application publication and patent as the illustration of the invention. Views must not be connected by projection lines and must not contain center lines. Applicant may suggest a single view (by figure number) for inclusion on the front page of the patent application publication and patent.

(i) **Scale.** The scale to which a drawing is made must be large enough to show the mechanism without crowding when the drawing is reduced in size to two-thirds in reproduction. Indications such as ``actual size'' or ``scale \1/2\'' on the drawings are not permitted since these lose their meaning with reproduction in a different format.

(j) **Character of lines, numbers, and letters.** All drawings must be made by a process which will give them satisfactory reproduction characteristics. Every line, number, and letter must be durable, clean, black (except for color drawings), sufficiently dense and dark, and uniformly thick and well defined. The weight of all lines and letters must be heavy enough to permit adequate reproduction. This requirement applies to all lines however fine, to shading, and to lines representing cut surfaces in sectional views. Lines and strokes of different thicknesses may be used in the same drawing where different thicknesses have a different meaning.

(k) **Shading.** The use of shading in views is encouraged if it aids in understanding the invention and if it does not reduce legibility. Shading is used to indicate the surface or shape of spherical, cylindrical, and conical elements of an object. Flat parts may also be lightly shaded. Such shading is preferred in the case of parts shown in perspective, but not for cross sections. See paragraph (h)(3) of this section. Spaced lines for shading are preferred. These lines must be thin, as few in number as practicable, and they must contrast with the rest of the drawings. As a substitute for shading, heavy lines on the shade side of objects can be used except where they superimpose on each other or obscure reference characters. Light should come from the upper left corner at an angle of 45°. Surface delineations should preferably be shown by proper shading. Solid black shading areas are not permitted, except when used to represent bar graphs or color.

(l) **Symbols.** Graphical drawing symbols may be used for conventional elements when appropriate. The elements for which such symbols and labeled representations are used must be adequately identified in the specification. Known devices should be illustrated by symbols that have a universally recognized conventional meaning and are generally accepted in the art. Other symbols which are not universally recognized may be used, subject to approval by the Office, if they are not likely to be confused with existing conventional symbols, and if they are readily identifiable.

(m) **Legends.** Suitable descriptive legends may be used subject to approval by the Office, or may be required by the examiner where necessary for understanding of the drawing. They should contain as few words as possible.

(n) **Numbers, letters, and reference characters.**

(1) Reference characters (numerals are preferred), sheet numbers, and view numbers must be plain and legible, and must not be used in association with brackets or inverted commas, or enclosed within outlines, e.g., encircled. They must be oriented in the same direction as the view so as to avoid having to rotate the sheet. Reference characters should be arranged to follow the profile of the object depicted.

(2) The English alphabet must be used for letters, except where another alphabet is customarily used, such as the Greek alphabet to indicate angles, wavelengths, and mathematical formulas.

(3) Numbers, letters, and reference characters must measure at least .32 cm. (1/8 inch) in height. They should not be placed in the drawing so as to interfere with its comprehension. Therefore, they should not cross or mingle with the lines. They should not be placed upon hatched or shaded surfaces. When necessary, such as indicating a surface or cross section, a reference character may be underlined and a blank space may be left in the hatching or shading where the character occurs so that it appears distinct.

(4) The same part of an invention appearing in more than one view of the drawing must always be designated by the same reference character, and the same reference character must never be used to designate different parts.

(5) Reference characters not mentioned in the description shall not appear in the drawings. Reference characters mentioned in the description must appear in the drawings.

(o) **Lead lines.** Lead lines are those lines between the reference characters and the details referred to. Such lines may be straight or curved and should be as short as possible. They must originate in the immediate proximity of the reference character and extend to the feature indicated. Lead lines must not cross each other. Lead lines are required for each reference character except for those which indicate the surface or cross section on which they are placed. Such a reference character must be underlined to make it clear that a lead line has not been left out by mistake. Lead lines must be executed in the same way as lines in the drawing. See paragraph (l) of this section.

(p) **Arrows.** Arrows may be used at the ends of lines, provided that their meaning is clear, as follows:
(1) On a lead line, a freestanding arrow to indicate the entire section towards which it points;

(2) On a lead line, an arrow touching a line to indicate the surface shown by the line looking along the direction of the arrow; or

(3) To show the direction of movement.

(q) **Copyright or Mask Work Notice.** A copyright or mask work notice may appear in the drawing, but must be placed within the sight of the drawing immediately below the figure representing the copyright or mask work material and be limited to letters having a print size of .32 cm. to .64 cm. (1/8 to 1/4 inches) high. The content of the notice must be limited to only those elements provided for by law. For example, "©1983 John Doe" (17 U.S.C. 401) and "*M* John Doe" (17 U.S.C. 909) would be properly limited and, under current statutes, legally sufficient notices of copyright and mask work, respectively. Inclusion of a copyright or mask work notice will be permitted only if the authorization language set forth in 1.71(e) is included at the beginning (preferably as the first paragraph) of the specification.

(r) **Numbering of sheets of drawings.** The sheets of drawings should be numbered in consecutive Arabic numerals, starting with 1, within the sight as defined in paragraph (g) of this section. These numbers, if present, must be placed in the middle of the top of the sheet, but not in the margin. The numbers can be placed on the right-hand side if the drawing extends too close to the middle of the top edge of the usable surface. The drawing sheet numbering must be clear and larger than the numbers used as reference characters to avoid confusion. The number of each sheet should be shown by two Arabic numerals placed on either side of an oblique line, with the first being the sheet number and the second being the total number of sheets of drawings, with no other marking.

(s) **Numbering of views.**

(1) The different views must be numbered in consecutive Arabic numerals, starting with 1, independent of the numbering of the sheets and, if possible, in the order in which they appear on the drawing sheet(s). Partial views intended to form one complete view, on one or several sheets, must be identified by the same number followed by a capital letter. View numbers must be preceded by the abbreviation "FIG." Where only a single view is used in an application to illustrate the claimed invention, it must not be numbered and the abbreviation "FIG." must not appear.

(2) Numbers and letters identifying the views must be simple and clear and must not be used in association with brackets, circles, or inverted commas. The view numbers must be larger than the numbers used for reference characters.

(t) **Security markings.** Authorized security markings may be placed on the drawings provided they are outside the sight, preferably centered in the top margin.

(u) **Corrections.** Any corrections on drawings submitted to the Office must be durable and permanent.

(v) **Holes.** No holes should be made by applicant in the drawing sheets.

(w) **Types of drawings.** See § 1.152 for design drawings, § 1.165 for plant drawings, and § 1.173(a)(2) for reissue drawings.

Models, Exhibits, And Specimens

Models or exhibits are not required in most patent applications since the description of the invention in the specification and the drawings must be sufficiently full, clear, and complete and capable of being understood to disclose the invention without the aid of a model.

A working model, or other physical exhibit, may be required by the Office if deemed necessary. This is not done very often. A working model may be requested in the case of applications for patent for alleged perpetual motion devices.

When the invention relates to a composition of matter, the applicant may be required to furnish specimens of the composition, or of its ingredients or intermediates, for inspection or experiment. If the invention is a microbiological invention, a deposit of the micro-organism involved is required.

Examination of Applications and Proceedings in the United States Patent and Trademark Office

Applications, other than provisional applications, filed in the United States Patent and Trademark Office (USPTO or Office) and accepted as complete applications are assigned for examination to the respective examining technology centers (TC) having charge of the areas of technology related to the invention. In the examining TC, applications are taken up for examination by the examiner to whom they have been assigned in the order in which they have been filed or in accordance with examining procedures established by the Director.

Applications will not be advanced out of turn for examination or for further action except as provided by the rules, or upon order of the Director to expedite the business of the Office, or upon a showing which, in the opinion of the Director, will justify advancing them.

The examination of the application consists of a study of the application for compliance with the legal requirements and a search through U.S. patents, publications of patent applications, foreign patent documents, and available literature, to see if the claimed invention is new, useful and nonobvious and if the application meets the requirements of the patent statute and rules of practice. If the examiner's decision on patentability is favorable, a patent is granted.

Restrictions

If two or more inventions are claimed in a single application, and are regarded by the Office to be of such a nature (e.g. independent and distinct) that a single patent should not be issued for both of them, the applicant will be required to limit the application to one of the inventions. The other invention may be made the subject of a separate application which, if filed while the first application is still pending, will be entitled to the benefit of the filing date of the first application. A requirement to restrict the application to one invention may be made before further action by the examiner.

Office Action

The applicant is notified in writing of the examiner's decision by an Office "action" which is normally mailed to the attorney or agent of record. The reasons for any adverse action or any objection or requirement are stated in the Office action and such information or references are given as may be useful in aiding the applicant to judge the propriety of continuing the prosecution of his/her application.

If the claimed invention is not directed to patentable subject matter, the claims will be rejected. If the examiner finds that the claimed invention lacks novelty or differs only in an obvious manner from what is found in the prior art, the claims may also be rejected. It is not uncommon for some or all of the claims to be rejected on the first Office action by the examiner; relatively few applications are allowed as filed.

Applicant's Reply

The applicant must request reconsideration in writing, and must distinctly and specifically point out the supposed errors in the examiner's Office action. The applicant must reply to every ground of objection and rejection in the prior Office action. The applicant's reply must appear throughout to be a bona fide attempt to advance the case to final action or allowance. The mere allegation that the examiner has erred will not be received as a proper reason for such reconsideration.

In amending an application in reply to a rejection, the applicant must clearly point out why he/she thinks the amended claims are patentable in view of the state of the art disclosed by the prior references cited or the objections made. He/she must also show how the claims as amended avoid such references or objections. After reply by the applicant, the application will be reconsidered, and the applicant will be notified as to the status of the claims, that is, whether the claims are rejected, or objected to, or whether the claims are allowed, in the same manner as after the first examination. The second Office action usually will be made final.

Interviews with examiners may be arranged, but an interview does not remove the necessity of replying to Office actions within the required time.

Final Rejection

On the second or later consideration, the rejection or other action may be made final. The applicant's reply is then limited to appeal in the case of rejection of any claim and further amendment is restricted. Petition may be taken to the Director in the case of objections or requirements not involved in the rejection of any claim. Reply to a final rejection or action must include cancellation of, or appeal from the rejection of, each claim so rejected and, if any claim stands allowed, compliance with any requirement or objection as to form. In making such final rejection, the examiner repeats or states all grounds of rejection then considered applicable to the claims in the application.

Amendments to Application

The applicant may amend the application as specified in the rules, or when and as specifically required by the examiner.

Amendments received in the Office on or before the mail date of the first Office action are called "preliminary amendments," and their entry is governed by 37 CFR 1.115. Amendments in reply to a non-final Office action are governed by CFR 1.111. Amendments filed after final action are governed by 37CFR 1.116 and 37CFR 41.33.

The specification, claims, and drawing must be amended and revised when required, to correct inaccuracies of description and definition or unnecessary words, and to provide substantial correspondence between the claims, the description, and the drawing. All amendments of the drawings or specification, and all additions thereto must not include new matter beyond the original disclosure. Matter not found in either, involving a departure from or an addition to the original disclosure, cannot be added to the application even if supported by a supplemental oath or declaration, and can be shown or claimed only in a separate application.

The manner of making amendments to an application is provided in 37 CFR 1.121. Amendments to the specification (but not including the claims) must be made by adding, deleting or replacing a paragraph, by replacing a section, or by a substitute specification, as provided in the rules. Replacement paragraphs are to include markings (e.g., underlining and strikethrough) to show all changes relative to the previous version of the paragraph. New paragraphs are to be provided without any underlining. If a substitute specification is filed, it must be submitted with markings (e.g., underlining and strikethrough) showing all the changes relative to the immediate prior version of the specification of record, it must be accompanied by a statement that the substitute specification includes no new matter, and it must be accompanied by a clean version without markings.

No change in the drawing may be made except by permission of the Office. Changes in the construction shown in any drawing may be made only by submitting replacement drawing sheets, each of which must be labeled "Replacement Sheet" in its top margin if replaces an existing drawing sheet. Any replacement sheet of drawings must include all of the figures appearing on the immediate prior version of the sheet, even if only one figure is amended. Any new sheet of drawings containing an additional figure must be labeled in the top margin as "New Sheet." All changes to the drawings must be explained, in detail, in either the drawing amendment or remarks section of the amendment paper.

Amendments to the claims are to be made by presenting all of the claims in a claim listing which replaces all prior versions of the claims in the application. In the claim listing, the status of every claim must be indicated after its claim number after using one of the seven parenthetical expressions set forth in 37 CFR 1.121(c). "Currently amended" claims must be submitted with markings (e.g., underlining and strikethrough). All pending claims not being currently amended must be presented in the claim listing in clean version without any markings (e.g., underlining and strikethrough).

The original numbering of the claims must be preserved throughout the prosecution. When claims are canceled, the remaining claims must not be renumbered. When claims are added by amendment or substituted for canceled claims, they must be numbered by the applicant consecutively beginning with the number next following the highest numbered claim previously presented. When the application is ready for allowance, the examiner, if necessary, will renumber the claims consecutively in the order in which they appear or in such order as may have been requested by applicant.

Time for Reply and Abandonment

The reply of an applicant to an action by the Office must be made within a prescribed time limit. The maximum period for reply is set at six months by the statute (35 U.S.C. 133) which also provides that the Director may shorten the time for reply to not less than 30 days. The usual period for reply to an Office action is three months. A shortened time for reply may be extended up to the maximum six-month period. An extension of time fee is normally required to be paid if the reply period is extended. The amount of the fee is dependent upon the length of the extension. Extensions of time are generally not available after an application has been allowed. If no reply is received within the time period, the application is considered as abandoned and no longer pending. However, if it can be shown that the failure to prosecute was unavoidable or unintentional, the application may be revived upon request to and approval by the Director. The revival requires a petition to the Director, and a fee for the petition, which must be filed without delay. The proper reply must also accompany the petition if it has not yet been filed.

Appeal to the Board of Patent Appeals and Interferences and to the Courts

If the examiner persists in the rejection of any of the claims in an application, or if the rejection has been made final, the applicant may appeal to the Board of Patent Appeals and Interferences in the United States Patent and Trademark Office. The Board of Patent Appeals and Interferences consists of the Under Secretary of Commerce for Intellectual Property and Director of the United States Patent and Trademark Office, the Deputy Under Secretary of Commerce for Intellectual Property and Deputy Director of the USPTO, the Commissioner for Patents, and the administrative patent judges, but normally each appeal is heard by only three members. An appeal fee is required and the applicant must file a brief to support his/her position. An oral hearing will be held if requested upon payment of the specified fee.

As an alternative to appeal, in situations where an applicant desires consideration of different claims or further evidence, a request for continued examination (RCE) or a continuation application is often filed. For the requirements for filing an RCE, see 37 CFR 1.114. An RCE is not available in an application for a design patent, but a continuation of a design application may be filed as a Continued Prosecution Application (CPA) under 37 CFR 1.53(d).

If the decision of the Board of Patent Appeals and Interferences is still adverse to the applicant, an appeal may be taken to the Court of Appeals for the Federal Circuit or a civil action may be filed against the Director in the United States District Court for the District of Columbia. The Court of Appeals for the Federal Circuit will review the record made in the Office and may affirm or reverse the Office's action. In a civil action, the applicant may present testimony in the court, and the court will make a decision.

Interferences

Occasionally two or more applications are filed by different inventors claiming substantially the same patentable invention. The patent can only be granted to one of them, and a proceeding known as "interference" is instituted by the Office to determine who is the first inventor and entitled to the patent. Less than one percent of the applications filed become involved in an interference proceeding. Interference proceedings may also be instituted between an application and a patent already issued, provided that the patent has not been issued, nor the application been published, for more than one year prior to the filing of the conflicting application, and provided also that the conflicting application is not barred from being patentable for some other reason.

Each party to such a proceeding must submit evidence of facts proving when the invention was made. In view of the necessity of proving the various facts and circumstances concerning the making of the invention during an interference, inventors must be able to produce evidence to do this. If no evidence is submitted a party is restricted to the date of filing the application as his/her earliest date. The priority question is determined by a board of three administrative patent judges on the evidence submitted. From the decision of the Board of Patent Appeals and Interferences, the losing party may appeal to the Court of Appeals for the Federal Circuit or file a civil action against the winning party in the appropriate United States district court.

The terms "conception of the invention" and "reduction to practice" are encountered in connection with priority questions. Conception of the invention refers to the completion of the devising of the means for accomplishing the result. Reduction to practice refers to the actual construction of the invention in physical form: in the case of a machine it includes the actual building of the machine, in the case of an article or composition it includes the actual making of the article or composition, in the case of a process it includes the actual carrying out of the steps of the process. Actual operation, demonstration, or testing for the intended use is also usually necessary. The filing of a regular application for patent completely disclosing the invention is treated as equivalent to reduction to practice. The inventor who proves to be the first to conceive the invention and the first to reduce it to practice will be held to be the prior inventor, but more complicated situations cannot be stated this simply.

Allowance and Issue of Patent

If, on examination of the application, or at a later stage during the reconsideration of the application, the patent application is found to be allowable, a Notice of Allowance and Fee(s) Due will be sent to the applicant, or to applicant's attorney or agent of record, if any, and a fee for issuing the patent and if applicable, for publishing the patent application publication (see 37 CFR 1.211-1.221), is due within three months from the date of the notice. If timely payment of the fee(s) is not made, the application will be regarded as abandoned. See the current fee schedule at ***www.uspto.gov***.

The Director may accept the fee(s) late, if the delay is shown to be unavoidable (35 U.S.C. 41, 37 CFR 1.137(a)) or unintentional (35 U.S.C. 151, 37 CFR 1.137(b)). When the required fees are paid, the patent issues as soon as possible after the date of payment, dependent upon the volume of printing on hand. The patent grant then is delivered or mailed on the day of its grant, or as soon thereafter as possible, to the inventor's attorney or agent if there is one of record, otherwise directly to the inventor. On the date of the grant, the patent file becomes open to the public for applications not opened earlier by publication of the application.

In cases where the publication of an application or the granting of a patent would be detrimental to the national security, the Commissioner of Patents will order that the invention be kept secret and shall withhold the publication of the application or the grant of the patent for such period as the national interest requires. The owner of an application which has been placed under a secrecy order has a right to appeal from the order to the Secretary of Commerce. 35 U.S.C. 181.

Patent Term Extension and Adjustment

The terms of certain patents may be subject to extension or adjustment under 35 U.S.C. 154(b). Such extension or adjustment results from certain specified types of delays which may occur while an application is pending before the Office.

Utility and plant patents which issue from original applications filed between June 8, 1995 and May 28, 2000 may be eligible for patent term extension (PTE) as set forth in 37 CFR 1.701. Such PTE may result from delays due to interference proceedings under 35 U.S.C. 135(a), secrecy orders under 35 U.S.C. 181, or successful appellate review.

Utility and plant patents which issue from original applications filed on or after May 29, 2000 may be eligible for patent term adjustment (PTA) as set forth in 37 CFR 1.702 – 1.705. There are three main bases for PTA under 35 U.S.C. 154(b). The first basis for PTA is the failure of the Office to take certain actions within specific time frames set forth in 35 U.S.C. 154(b)(1)(A) (See 37 CFR 1.702(a) and 1.703(a)). The second basis for PTA is the failure of the Office to issue a patent within three years of the actual filing date of the application as set forth in 35 U.S.C. 154(b)(1)(B) (See 37 CFR 1.702(b) and 1.703(b)). The third basis for PTA is set forth in 35 U.S.C. 154(b)(1)(C), and includes delays due to interference proceedings under 35 U.S.C. 135(a), secrecy orders under 35 U.S.C. 181, or successful appellate review (See 37 CFR 1.702(c)-(e) and 1.703(c)-(e)).

Any PTA which has accrued in an application will be reduced by the time period during which an applicant failed to engage in reasonable efforts to conclude prosecution of the application pursuant to 35 U.S.C. 154(b)(2)(C). A non-exclusive list of activities which constitute failure to engage in reasonable efforts to conclude prosecution is set forth in 37 CFR 1.704.

An initial PTA value is printed on the notice of allowance and fee(s) due, and a final PTA value is printed on the front of the patent. Any request for reconsideration of the PTA value printed on the notice of allowance and fee(s) due should be made in the form of an application for patent term adjustment, which must be filed prior to or at the same time as the payment of the issue fee. (See 37 CFR 1.705.)

Nature of Patent and Patent Rights

The patent is issued in the name of the United States under the seal of the United States Patent and Trademark Office, and is either signed by the Director of the USPTO or is electronically written thereon and attested by an Office official. The patent contains a grant to the patentee, and a printed copy of the specification and drawing is annexed to the patent and forms a part of it. The grant confers "the right to exclude others from making, using, offering for sale, or selling the invention throughout the United States or importing the invention into the United States" and its territories and possessions for which the term of the patent shall be generally 20 years from the date on which the application for the patent was filed in the United States or, if the application contains a specific reference to an earlier filed application under 35 U.S.C. 120, 121 or 365(c), from the date of the earliest such application was filed, and subject to the payment of maintenance fees as provided by law.

The exact nature of the right conferred must be carefully distinguished, and the key is in the words "right to exclude" in the phrase just quoted. The patent does not grant the right to make, use, offer for sale or sell or import the invention but only grants the exclusive nature of the right. Any person is ordinarily free to make, use, offer for sale or sell or import anything he/she pleases, and a grant from the government is not necessary. The patent only grants the right to exclude others from making, using, offering for sale or selling or importing the invention. Since the patent does not grant the right to make, use, offer for sale, or sell, or import the invention, the patentee's own right to do so is dependent upon the rights of others and whatever general laws might be applicable. A patentee, merely because he/she has received a patent for an invention, is not thereby authorized to make, use, offer for sale, or sell, or import the invention if doing so would violate any law.

An inventor of a new automobile who has obtained a patent thereon would not be entitled to use the patented automobile in violation of the laws of a state requiring a license, nor may a patentee sell an article, the sale of which may be forbidden by a law, merely because a patent has been obtained. Neither may a patentee make, use, offer for sale, or sell, or import his/her own invention if doing so would infringe the prior rights of others. A patentee may not violate the federal antitrust laws, such as by resale price agreements or entering into combination in restraints of trade, or the pure food and drug laws, by virtue of having a patent. Ordinarily there is nothing that prohibits a patentee from making, using, offering for sale, or selling, or importing his/her own invention, unless he/she thereby infringes another's patent which is still in force. For example, a patent for an improvement of an original device already patented would be subject to the patent on the device.

The term of the patent shall be generally 20 years from the date on which the application for the patent was filed in the United States or, if the application contains a specific reference to an earlier filed application under 35 U.S.C. 120, 121 or 365(c), from the date of the earliest such application was filed, and subject to the payment of maintenance fees as provided by law. A maintenance fee is due 3 1/2, 7 1/2 and 11 1/2 years after the original grant for all patents issuing from the applications filed on and after December 12, 1980. The maintenance fee must be paid at the stipulated times to maintain the patent in force. After the patent has expired anyone may make, use, offer for sale, or sell or import the invention without permission of the patentee, provided that matter covered by other unexpired patents is not used. The terms may be extended for certain pharmaceuticals and for certain circumstances as provided by law.

Maintenance Fees

All utility patents that issue from applications filed on or after December 12, 1980 are subject to the payment of maintenance fees which must be paid to maintain the patent in force. These fees are due at 3 1/2, 7 1/2 and 11 1/2 years from the date the patent is granted and can be paid without a surcharge during the "window-period" which is the six-month period preceding each due date, e.g., three years to three years and six months. (See fee schedule for a list of maintenance fees.) In submitting maintenance fees and any necessary surcharges, identification of the patents for which maintenance fees are being paid must include the patent number, and the application number of the U.S. application for the patent on which the maintenance fee is being paid. If the payment includes identification of only the patent number, the Office may apply payment to the patent identified by patent number in the payment or the Office may return the payment. (See 37, Code of Federal Regulations, section 1.366(c).)

Failure to pay the current maintenance fee on time may result in expiration of the patent. A six-month grace period is provided when the maintenance fee may be paid with a surcharge. The grace period is the six-month period immediately following the due date. The USPTO does not mail notices to patent owners that maintenance fees are due. If, however, the maintenance fee is not paid on time, efforts are made to remind the responsible party that the maintenance fee may be paid during the grace period with a surcharge. If the maintenance fee is not paid on time and the maintenance fee and surcharge are not paid during the grace period, the patent expires on the date the grace period ends.

Correction of Patents

Once the patent is granted, it is outside the jurisdiction of the USPTO except in a few respects. The Office may issue without charge a certificate correcting a clerical error it has made in the patent when the printed patent does not correspond to the record in the Office. These are mostly corrections of typographical errors made in printing. Some minor errors of a typographical nature made by the applicant may be corrected by a certificate of correction for which a fee is required. The patentee may disclaim one or more claims of his/her patent by filing in the Office a disclaimer as provided by the statute (35 U.S.C. 253).

When the patent is defective in certain respects, the law provides that the patentee may apply for a reissue patent. Following an examination in which the proposed changes correcting any defects in the original patent are evaluated, a reissue patent would be granted to replace the original and is granted only for the balance of the unexpired term. However, the nature of the changes that can be made by means of the reissue are rather limited; new matter cannot be added. In a different type of proceeding, any person may file a request for reexamination of a patent, along with the required fee, on the basis of prior art consisting of patents or printed publications. At the conclusion of the reexamination proceedings, a certificate setting forth the results of the reexamination proceeding is issued.

Assignments and Licenses

A patent is personal property and may be sold to others or mortgaged; it may be bequeathed by a will; and it may pass to the heirs of a deceased patentee. The patent law provides for the transfer or sale of a patent, or of an application for patent, by an instrument in writing. Such an instrument is referred to as an assignment and may transfer the entire interest in the patent. The assignee, when the patent is assigned to him or her, becomes the owner of the patent and has the same rights that the original patentee had.

The statute also provides for the assignment of a part interest, that is, a half interest, a fourth interest, etc., in a patent. There may also be a grant that conveys the same character of interest as an assignment but only for a particularly specified part of the United States. A mortgage of patent property passes ownership thereof to the mortgagee or lender until the mortgage has been satisfied and a retransfer from the mortgagee back to the mortgagor, the borrower, is made. A conditional assignment also passes ownership of the patent and is regarded as absolute until canceled by the parties or by the decree of a competent court.

An assignment, grant, or conveyance of any patent or application for patent should be acknowledged before a notary public or officer authorized to administer oaths or perform notarial acts. The certificate of such acknowledgment constitutes prima facie evidence of the execution of the assignment, grant, or conveyance.

Recording of Assignments

The Office records assignments, grants, and similar instruments sent to it for recording, and the recording serves as notice. If an assignment, grant, or conveyance of a patent or an interest in a patent (or an application for patent) is not recorded in the Office within three months from its date, it is void against a subsequent purchaser for a valuable consideration without notice, unless it is recorded prior to the subsequent purchase.

An instrument relating to a patent should identify the patent by number and date (the name of the inventor and title of the invention as stated in the patent should also be given). An instrument relating to an application should identify the application by its application number and date of filing, the name of the inventor, and title of the invention as stated in the application should also be given. Sometimes an assignment of an application is executed at the same time that the application is prepared and before it has been filed in the Office. Such assignment should adequately identify the application, as by its date of execution and name of the inventor and title of the invention, so that there can be no mistake as to the application intended. If an application has been assigned and the assignment has been recorded or filed for recordation, the patent will be issued to the assignee as owner, if the name of the assignee is provided when the issue fee is paid and the patent is requested to be issued to the assignee. If the assignment is of a part interest only, the patent will be issued to the inventor and assignee as joint owners.

Joint Ownership

Patents may be owned jointly by two or more persons as in the case of a patent granted to joint inventors, or in the case of the assignment of a part interest in a patent. Any joint owner of a patent, no matter how small the part interest, may make, use, offer for sale and sell and import the invention for his or her own profit provided they do not infringe another's patent rights, without regard to the other owners, and may sell the interest or any part of it, or grant licenses to others, without regard to the other joint owner, unless the joint owners have made a contract governing their relation to each other. It is accordingly dangerous to assign a part interest without a definite agreement between the parties as to the extent of their respective rights and their obligations to each other if the above result is to be avoided.

The owner of a patent may grant licenses to others. Since the patentee has the right to exclude others from making, using, offering for sale, or selling or importing the invention, no one else may do any of these things without his/her permission.

A patent license agreement is in essence nothing more than a promise by the licensor not to sue the licensee. No particular form of license is required; a license is a contract and may include whatever provisions the parties agree upon, including the payment of royalties, etc.
The drawing up of a license agreement (as well as assignments) is within the field of an attorney at law. Such attorney should be familiar with patent matters as well. A few States have prescribed certain formalities to be observed in connection with the sale of patent rights.

Infringement of Patents

Infringement of a patent consists of the unauthorized making, using, offering for sale, or selling any patented invention within the United States or U.S. Territories, or importing into the United States of any patented invention during the term of the patent. If a patent is infringed, the patentee may sue for relief in the appropriate federal court. The patentee may ask the court for an injunction to prevent the continuation of the infringement and may also ask the court for an award of damages because of the infringement. In such an infringement suit, the defendant may raise the question of the validity of the patent, which is then decided by the court. The defendant may also aver that what is being done does not constitute infringement. Infringement is determined primarily by the language of the claims of the patent and, if what the defendant is making does not fall within the language of any of the claims of the patent, there is no literal infringement.

Suits for infringement of patents follow the rules of procedure of the federal courts. From the decision of the district court, there is an appeal to the Court of Appeals for the Federal Circuit. The Supreme Court may thereafter take a case by writ of certiorari. If the United States Government infringes a patent, the patentee has a remedy for damages in the United States Court of Federal Claims. The government may use any patented invention without permission of the patentee, but the patentee is entitled to obtain compensation for the use by or for the government. The Office has no jurisdiction over questions relating to infringement of patents. In examining applications for patent, no determination is made as to whether the invention sought to be patented infringes any prior patent. An improvement invention may be patentable, but it might infringe a prior unexpired patent for the invention improved upon, if there is one.

Patent Marking and Patent Pending

A patentee who makes or sells patented articles, or a person who does so for or under the patentee is required to mark the articles with the word "Patent" and the number of the patent. The penalty for failure to mark is that the patentee may not recover damages from an infringer unless the infringer was duly notified of the infringement and continued to infringe after the notice.

The marking of an article as patented when it is not in fact patented is against the law and subjects the offender to a penalty. Some persons mark articles sold with the terms "Patent Applied For" or "Patent Pending." These phrases have no legal effect, but only give information that an application for patent has been filed in the USPTO. The protection afforded by a patent does not start until the actual grant of the patent. False use of these phrases or their equivalent is prohibited.

Design Patents

The patent laws provide for the granting of design patents to any person who has invented any new and nonobvious ornamental design for an article of manufacture. The design patent protects only the appearance of an article, but not its structural or functional features. The proceedings relating to granting of design patents are the same as those relating to other patents with a few differences. See current fee schedule for the filing fee for a design application. A design patent has a term of 14 years from grant, and no fees are necessary to maintain a design patent in force. If on examination it is determined that an applicant is entitled to a design patent under the law, a notice of allowance will be sent to the applicant or applicant's attorney, or agent, calling for the payment of an issue fee. The drawing of the design patent conforms to the same rules as other drawings, but no reference characters are allowed and the drawing should clearly depict the appearance, since the drawing defines the scope of patent protection.
The specification of a design application is short and ordinarily follows a set form. Only one claim is permitted, following a set form that refers to the drawing(s).

Plant Patents

The law also provides for the granting of a patent to anyone who has invented or discovered and asexually reproduced any distinct and new variety of plant, including cultivated sports, mutants, hybrids, and newly found seedlings, other than a tuber-propagated plant or a plant found in an uncultivated state.

Asexually propagated plants are those that are reproduced by means other than from seeds, such as by the rooting of cuttings, by layering, budding, grafting, inarching, etc.

With reference to tuber-propagated plants, for which a plant patent cannot be obtained, the term "tuber" is used in its narrow horticultural sense as meaning a short, thickened portion of an underground branch. Such plants covered by the term "tuber-propagated" are the Irish potato and the Jerusalem artichoke.

An application for a plant patent consists of the same parts as other applications. The term of a plant patent shall be 20 years from the date on which the application for the patent was filed in the United States or, if the application contains a specific reference to an earlier filed application under 35 U.S.C. 120, 121 or 365(c), from the date the earliest such application was filed.

The specification should include a complete detailed description of the plant and the characteristics thereof that distinguish the same over related known varieties, and its antecedents, expressed in botanical terms in the general form followed in standard botanical text books or publications dealing with the varieties of the kind of plant involved (evergreen tree, dahlia plant, rose plant, apple tree, etc.), rather than a mere broad non-botanical characterization such as commonly found in nursery or seed catalogs. The specification should also include the origin or parentage of the plant variety sought to be patented and must particularly point out where and in what manner the variety of plant has been asexually reproduced. The Latin name of the genus and species of the plant should be stated. Where color is a distinctive feature of the plant, the color should be positively identified in the specification by reference to a designated color as given by a recognized color dictionary. Where the plant variety originated as a newly found seedling, the specification must fully describe the conditions (cultivation, environment, etc.) under which the seedling was found growing to establish that it was not found in an uncultivated state.

A plant patent is granted on the entire plant. It therefore follows that only one claim is necessary and only one is permitted.

The oath or declaration required of the applicant in addition to the statements required for other applications must include the statement that the applicant has asexually reproduced the new plant variety. If the plant is a newly found plant, the oath or declaration must also state that the plant was found in a cultivated area.

Plant patent drawings are not mechanical drawings and should be artistically and competently executed. The drawing must disclose all the distinctive characteristics of the plant capable of visual representation. When color is a distinguishing characteristic of the new variety, the drawing must be in color. Two duplicate copies of color drawings must be submitted. All color drawings should include a one-inch margin at the top for Office markings when the patent is printed.

Specimens of the plant variety, its flower or fruit, should not be submitted unless specifically called for by the examiner.

The filing fee on each plant application and the issue fee can be found in the fee schedule. For a qualifying small entity most fees are reduced by half. 35 U.S.C. 41(h)(1). Plant patent applications may be published pursuant to Title 35, United States Code, Section 122(b), but the publication fee is not reduced for small entities.

A plant patent application is the only type of patent application filed at the USPTO which is not permitted to be filed via EFS-Web.

All inquiries relating to plant patents and pending plant patent applications should be directed to the United States Patent and Trademark Office and not to the Department of Agriculture.

The Plant Variety Protection Act (Public Law 91577), approved December 24, 1970, provides for a system of protection for sexually reproduced varieties, for which protection was not previously provided, under the administration of a Plant Variety Protection Office within the Department of Agriculture. Requests for information regarding the protection of sexually reproduced varieties should be addressed to Commissioner, Plant Variety Protection Office, Agricultural Marketing Service, National Agricultural Library Bldg., Room 0, 10301 Baltimore Blvd., Beltsville, Md. 20705-2351.

Treaties and Foreign Patents

Since the rights granted by a U.S. patent extend only throughout the territory of the United States and have no effect in a foreign country, an inventor who wishes patent protection in other countries must apply for a patent in each of the other countries or in regional patent offices. Almost every country has its own patent law, and a person desiring a patent in a particular country must make an application for patent in that country, in accordance with the requirements of that country.

The laws of many countries differ in various respects from the patent law of the United States. In most foreign countries, publication of the invention before the date of the application will bar the right to a patent. Most foreign countries require that the patented invention must be manufactured in that country after a certain period, usually three years. If there is no manufacture within this period, the patent may be void in some countries, although in most countries the patent may be subject to the grant of compulsory licenses to any person who may apply for a license.

There is a treaty relating to patents which is adhered to by 169 countries, including the United States, and is known as the Paris Convention for the Protection of Industrial Property. It provides that each country guarantees to the citizens of the other countries the same rights in patent and trademark matters that it gives to its own citizens. The treaty also provides for the right of priority in the case of patents, trademarks and industrial designs (design patents). This right means that, on the basis of a regular first application filed in one of the member countries, the applicant may, within a certain period of time, apply for protection in all the other member countries. These later applications will then be regarded as if they had been filed on the same day as the first application. Thus, these later applicants will have priority over applications for the same invention that may have been filed during the same period of time by other persons. Moreover, these later applications, being based on the first application, will not be invalidated by any acts accomplished in the interval, such as, for example, publication or exploitation of the invention, the sale of copies of the design, or use of the trademark. The period of time mentioned above, within which the subsequent applications may be filed in the other countries, is 12 months in the case of first applications for patent and six months in the case of industrial designs and trademarks.

Another treaty, known as the Patent Cooperation Treaty, was negotiated at a diplomatic conference in Washington, D.C., in June of 1970. The treaty came into force on January 24, 1978, and is presently (as of March 29, 2005) adhered to by over 126 countries, including the United States. The treaty facilitates the filing of applications for patent on the same invention in member countries by providing, among other things, for centralized filing procedures and a standardized application format.

The timely filing of an international application affords applicants an international filing date in each country which is designated in the international application and provides (1) a search of the invention and (2) a later time period within which the national applications for patent must be filed. A number of patent attorneys specialize in obtaining patents in foreign countries.

Under U.S. law it is necessary, in the case of inventions made in the United States, to obtain a license from the Director of the USPTO before applying for a patent in a foreign country. Such a license is required if the foreign application is to be filed before an application is filed in the United States or before the expiration of six months from the filing of an application in the United States unless a filing receipt with a license grant issued earlier. The filing of an application for a U.S. patent constitutes the request for a license and the granting or denial of such request is indicated in the filing receipt mailed to each applicant. After six months from the U.S. filing, a license is not required unless the invention has been ordered to be kept secret. If the invention has been ordered to be kept secret, the consent to the filing abroad must be obtained from the Director of the USPTO during the period the order of secrecy is in effect.

Foreign Applicants for U.S. Patents

The patent laws of the United States make no discrimination with respect to the citizenship of the inventor. Any inventor, regardless of his/her citizenship, may apply for a patent on the same basis as a U.S. citizen. There are, however, a number of particular points of special interest to applicants located in foreign countries.

The application for patent in the United States must be made by the inventor and the inventor must sign the oath or declaration (with certain exceptions), differing from the law in many countries where the signature of the inventor and an oath of inventorship are not necessary. If the inventor is dead, the application may be made by his/her executor or administrator, or equivalent, and in the case of mental disability it may be made by his/her legal representative (guardian).

No U.S. patent can be obtained if the invention was patented abroad before applying in the United States by the inventor or his/her legal representatives if the foreign application was filed more than 12 months before filing in the United States. Six months are allowed in the case of designs. 35 U.S.C. 172.

An application for a patent filed in the United States by any person who has previously regularly filed an application for a patent for the same invention in a foreign country which affords similar privileges to citizens of the United States shall have the same force and effect for the purpose of overcoming intervening acts of others as if filed in the United States on the date on which the application for a patent for the same invention was first filed in such foreign country. This is the case, provided the application in the United States is filed within 12 months (six months in the case of a design patent) from the earliest date on which any such foreign application was filed and claims priority under 35 U.S.C. 119(b) to the foreign application. A copy of the foreign application certified by the patent office of the country in which it was filed is required to secure this right of priority.

If any application for patent has been filed in any foreign country by the applicant or by his/her legal representatives or assigns prior to his/her application in the United States, in order to claim priority under 35 U.S.C. 119(b) to the foreign application, the applicant must, in the oath or declaration accompanying the application, state the country in which the earliest such application has been filed, giving the date of filing the application. If foreign priority is claimed, any foreign application having a filing date before that of the application on which priority is claimed must also be identified in the oath or declaration. Where no claim for foreign priority under 35 U.S.C. 119(b) is made in the U.S. application, the applicant should identify in the oath or declaration those foreign applications disclosing similar inventions filed more than a year before the filing in the United States.

An oath or alternatively a declaration must be made with respect to every application. When the applicant is in a foreign country the oath or affirmation may be before any diplomatic or consular officer of the United States, or before any officer having an official seal and authorized to administer oaths in the foreign country, whose authority shall be proved by a certificate of a diplomatic or consular officer of the United States. The oath is attested in all cases by the proper official seal of the officer before whom the oath is made.

When the oath is taken before an officer in the country foreign to the United States, all the application papers (except the drawing) must be attached together and a ribbon passed one or more times through all the sheets of the application, and the ends of the ribbons brought together under the seal before the latter is affixed and impressed, or each sheet must be impressed with the official seal of the officer before whom the oath was taken. A declaration merely requires the use of a specific averment found in 37 CFR 1.68.

If the application is filed by the legal representative (executor, administrator, etc.) of a deceased inventor, the legal representative must make the oath or declaration. When a declaration is used, the ribboning procedure is not necessary, nor is it necessary to appear before an official in connection with the making of a declaration.

A foreign applicant may be represented by any patent attorney or agent who is registered to practice before the United States Patent and Trademark Office.

www.ingramcontent.com/pod-product-compliance
Lightning Source LLC
Chambersburg PA
CBHW081812170526
45167CB00008B/3408